TREASURE HUNT
YOUR CITY

Treasure Hunt Your City

NEW EXPERIENCES TO DISCOVER YOUR SELF-CONFIDENCE

Jennifer Erickson, Ph.D.

Jennifer Erickson Arts

Contents

Dedication	vii
One Why Is This A Treasure Hunt?	2
Two Low Self-Confidence	6
Three Prepare for the Experience	8
Four Clue One – A new culinary experience	12
Five Clue two – Get wild	18
Six clue Three – smell the Flowers	23
Seven clue four – Step away from the Asphalt	28
Eight clue Five – Walk in History	33
Nine Clue Six – wait for sunset	38
Ten Clue Seven – Test a Hobby	43

Eleven
Clue Eight – find a quiet place   49

Twelve
clue Nine – Go low Tech   55

Thirteen
clue Ten – See the world Differently   60

Fourteen
clue ELEVEN – be fruity   65

Fifteen
Clue twelve – find your Season   70

Sixteen
finding your TREASURE   76

About The Author   81

To my partner Steve and to my mother. You two have been the biggest supporters of my personal and professional journey. I wouldn't be able to help others if it weren't for you two helping me. Thank you.

Copyright © 2021 by Jennifer Erickson

All rights reserved. No part of this book may be reproduced in any manner whatsoever without written permission except in the case of brief quotations embodied in critical articles and reviews.

Designed by Hannah Gaskamp
Photography by Jennifer Erickson

First Printing, 2021
JenniferEricksonArts.com

Acknowledgement

I have to start by thanking my mother, Terry. From the time I started my new personal and professional journey you have helped. You've taken time to review my websites, business cards, book drafts, and this workbook is no exception. Your time editing and offering advice was invaluable.

I also want to thank the people in my life who encouraged me to create the workbook. It is through countless conversations with people, trying to help people on their self-confidence journey, that the many ideas for this workbook came to be. I hope we can all help support each other and through gaining self-confidence, can live happier and more fulfilling lives.

One

Why Is This A Treasure Hunt?

    I selected the title of this workbook as Treasure Hunt Your City because humans thrive on fun, on adventure, and on exploration. In fact, in child development, basic play is necessary for healthy development because it helps encourage problem solving, it helps us learn to test ideas, it helps us to learn cooperation and teamwork. Children love to treasure hunt because it takes "change", and "self-confidence", and "brainstorming" to a fun and fearless level. Isn't it interesting that as adults, we tend to lose those skills?

    Just like when we were children, we need to re-access those moments where we didn't judge ourselves, where we didn't doubt ourselves, and where we didn't fear failure. As a child is treasure hunting, they think out loud, they get it wrong, they try and try again. And rarely do they think, "I'm a terrible person because I can't figure it out". This is why it is time to treasure hunt again. We need to laugh at ourselves, we need to fail and try and try again, we need to seek an adventure. And through this process we can begin to gain self-confidence.

What is self-confidence? It is a feeling of trust in one's abilities, qualities, and judgement. Yes, it is normal to lose self-confidence at times. But when we lose it repeatedly, it can be hard to gain it back. We begin to focus on self-doubt, past failures, and inadequacies.

Today I challenge you. Don't get caught in one mindset. I challenge you to go find your clues. I challenge you to have new experiences. I challenge you to fail and try and try again. I challenge you to trust in yourself. With all of that, you may find your treasure.

Are you asking yourself, "but what is the treasure?" That is a good question. You will know your treasure when you find it. The treasure here, is finding your authentic self. Is this a new term for you? I love this term. What it means to find your authentic self is to know truly who you are as a person, regardless of your occupation, regardless of the influences of others, it is an honest representation of you. To be authentic means to not care what others think about you. To be authentic means to be true to yourself through your words, thoughts, and actions.

I hope you are now asking, "well, how does someone become authentic". The answer is, through experiences and reflection. Through experience and reflection, we become more in tune with who we are. Let me give you an example. If from the time you were a toddler to the time you were twenty two, your parents, aunts and uncles, and even teachers said to you, "don't eat broccoli, it is bad for you, it will upset your stomach, its gross, etc". I bet I can guess how you would feel about broccoli. Now I'm only picking on broccoli because it's a food I used to think was not tasty, but through experience, through trying it in many forms, I have come to love broccoli and enjoy eating it. My true self is a person who would eat broccoli with any meal. Okay, maybe not breakfast.

I hope you understand my point. When we are younger, we were influenced by people around us. This is very normal. This is how information, culture, religion, and so much more is passed from generation to generation. But as we get older, we don't test the ideology, the beliefs, and the knowledge that was given to us, we might be unsure of ourselves. We might always wonder why. We gain confidence in ourselves when we take the knowledge that was shared, and then we experience it. We determine for ourselves how we feel about something, what we believe in, and what our values are.

We gain confidence in our beliefs through experience. So, to re-gain lost confidence, we must start on a new journey of personal growth. We need to access that younger free spirit that is still within us. Our treasure can only be discovered by experiences that allow us to reflect and grow. It does not mean we have to do everything alone. It just means that when you have a new experience, you need to reflect on it, determine what you believe and how you feel about it, and then feel okay to share your beliefs with the person who is on this experience with you. This way you know your opinion is not influence by the person you are with.

What I recommend is that you go into this journey with an open mind. Try some of the adventures by yourself (always with safety first). Try some of the experiences with a friend. Try some of the experience in a way that costs no money. And try some of the experience in a way that has a fee. Try some of the experiences in your home and try some of the experiences out in the world (again, safety first). Be open to the full experience and then write down as much as you remember. The goal is to not necessarily enjoy each experience. That might be a bonus. But the goal is to learn, to self-grow, through each experience.

The variety of clues in this workbook take you on a variation of journeys that should be available in most cities. I presently live in Richmond, Virginia. I reference some places and ideas that can be completed in Richmond to give you some ideas of what you might find in your city. While I do believe that cities offer different things to different people, you should be able to find "you" wherever you go.

I wish you a great time on this adventure.

Two

Low Self-Confidence

First what is self-confidence? It is typically defined as an inward attitude about your own skills and abilities. That inward attitude is normally positive with you accepting and trusting yourself. It is having self-awareness in your own strengths and abilities. An example might be someone who plays the piano and is able to acknowledge to themselves that they are able to play a song well.

Why is self-confidence so important? It allows you to express yourself authentically, it allows you freedom from draining self-doubt, and helps prevent negative thoughts about yourself. It doesn't mean that you become arrogant, which is a fear that many people have. Being arrogant is a state where people have an exaggerated sense of ones' own abilities. Self-confidence is an inward belief rather than an outward expression. However, when someone has self-confidence, they can assert themselves and their needs, in a way that is strong, and respectful to the boundaries of others.

What is daily life like when we struggle with low self-confidence? Well, many people with low self-confidence also have low self-esteem. They tend to be generally more negative in their perceptions about themselves and their ability to succeed in life. There is an innate disadvantage to low self-confidence. People tend to struggle more in areas of commitment, determination, and perseverance. These attributes are necessary to make progress in areas of life, especially personal growth.

With struggles in personal growth, we might not set boundaries with our jobs, with relationships, with people in general. We might not believe we are worthy of these boundaries. This can lead to feelings of inadequacy, fear, and uneasiness.

Confidence is a belief that comes out of appreciating one's own abilities or qualities.

Your treasure is waiting for you. This workbook may not take you to the end of your journey. In all honesty, I hope it creates momentum for a lifelong journey of personal growth and awareness.

Three

Prepare for the Experience

Are you ready to start your treasure hunt? You might be feeling a bit anxious, and that is okay. Do you know what anxiousness is? In simplest terms, it is a feeling of worry, nervousness, or unease, typically about an imminent event or something with an uncertain outcome. What do you think about the general definition? Why do you think I want you to know the definition of anxiety? (pause for thought)

Because I want you to know that it is okay and normal to "feel" both physically and emotionally a bit uneasy about trying new things. The physical comes from the adrenaline response system tied to the "fight or flight" response. Typical symptoms related to the adrenaline response are rapid heartbeat, high blood pressure, expanding the air passages of the lungs, enlarging the pupils in the eyes to see, redistributing blood to the muscles, excess sweating and palpitations, altering the body's metabolism to maximize blood glucose levels (primarily for the brain), and a few more things happen. Think about all of these changes that the body goes through as a result of the adrenaline response due to fear. The important thing to remember is, this is all normal and your body is used to it.

When there is a legitimate fear response; there is actually a danger issue. We tend to not notice the physical response as much because we are focused on the danger. We might notice it later and I've found that most people don't judge it, people deem it normal due to the danger or fear. However, when the fear is cognitive (fear based on the way we perceive something), we tend to notice the physical response so much more, and then we tend to "fear" the fear response. This is where a lot of anxiety actually comes from.

Going back to the second paragraph, I want you to know what anxiety is, what nervousness is, so that you don't fear it. I just talked about how it "feels" physically to try something new. Let's talk about how it can "feel" emotionally. Many people feel emotionally uneasy trying something new, because of words like anxiety, we stop trying to experience something new. "We don't want our anxiety to get out of control". But let's dig deeper into our emotional words.

When I ask people to stop using the word "anxiety" and to select more specific words, the typical words that are used are: vulnerable, inferior, insecure, exposed, worried, and maybe even helpless. It is important to dig deeper and ask yourself why you feel YOUR more specific words. Since this not a counseling workbook, if you struggle with any of YOUR emotional words, definitely find a therapist or psychologist to talk to. My disclaimer to you is, it is better to stop and talk to a therapist about your anxiety, and then start working on the workbook, if you have excessive worry.

Moving forward with this workbook, what you need to know is that it is okay to feel nervous, to feel vulnerable, to feel inexperienced. In fact, this may be what you are if you haven't done a whole lot of things on your own. Hence, the feeling of low confidence. Experience gives us a chance to learn, to reflect, and to become more familiar with people, places, events, and things.

All of this information can hopefully help you prepare for your experiences, for your treasure hunts. Know and accept, you might have an adrenaline response (it will pass). Know and accept you might feel emotionally vulnerable, nervous, inexperienced or many other emotion words. Don't fear these feelings, rather embrace them because each treasure hunt you complete gives you experience, can reduce nerves, and can help you feel less vulnerable. So the experiences themselves, help resolve the "fear" feelings.

Another way to prepare for your treasure hunt is to really give each of the items some thought. Don't just jump at the first idea you have. It is highly recommended that you do some alone. When you do some of them alone, it is important to feel safe. For example, I never recommend to any person, to hike alone. So, if you decide to walk a trail, walk with a buddy. Always safety first.

Another way to prepare, when you experience a "clue" by going on a hike, sitting at the beach, watching a sunset, and many of the others, make sure you have supplies with you if needed. What I mean by supplies is, if it is hot, have your water bottles, if the distance is a drive, make sure you prepare to eat. Please make sure you consider the entire experience (going there, being there, and coming home) to ensure that it is the best that it can be.

One final recommendation. If you bring a friend to go with you, because some of these are nice to experience with someone, make sure you ask them to not share their thoughts until you get to write yours down. The goal is for you to be able to have the experience and reflect on it, without the influence of another. Once you have written down your thoughts, then ask them how the experience was for them. Learn how you had similar and different experiences for the same event. This is a great way to understand your friend better, understand how unique individuals are, and that it is okay for two people to feel differently about an experience.

Last item. Make sure you have this workbook, so you can write down your thoughts. Don't forget a pen or pencil. And if you need, something hard to write on. Go through the experience with an open mind. And reflect in each chapter honestly. Its hard to learn yourself if you are not being honest with yourself.

I don't expect you to like all of your experiences. That would be unrealistic. I hope you gain some personal perspective, personal insight, and personal awareness with each experience. That is how you can eventually find your treasure; your confidence in yourself and in your judgement.

Enjoy the hunt.

Four

Clue One – A new culinary experience

Food is an essential part of our life. We eat several times a day (matching our personal goals). Food is not just for nutrition though; many cultures include food in their social gatherings, and many people use food for social connectedness. It is this aspect that can cause angst for people with social anxiety. And that is why practicing experiences is so important. Whether you are struggling with confidence, you are shy/introverted, or just inexperienced with culinary diversity, this is a great confidence builder.

Let's talk about what the culinary experience might look like. First, I would say, try a restaurant, café, diner, etc. Basically, some place you must eat out. Does this make you cringe? If yes, then you know it is the right challenge. You can go with a friend if it helps, but I really recommend going by yourself at some point. When I suggest this to people, they will often look at me as if to say, "but people eating alone look so sad". My response is typically, "that is your projection because of your fears or insecurities". There is no judgement in eating alone and remember not everyone is comfortable in new situations. I respect that. AND it can also prevent us from fully gaining inner confidence.

So, no judgement and no projecting fears. If you do go with a friend, just ask them to not share their thoughts about the experience until you have had a chance to collect your thoughts and make notes. If they have a different experience, that is okay, we are all unique and we will reflect on things differently.

After your experience dining out, try an experience eating in. Pick a recipe and cook something new. My favorite is homemade apple pie. Okay, I don't make the crust from scratch, but everything else. I have also baked stuffed shells; seafood is something I learned how to cook. And during the holidays, I love cooking my grandmothers fudge. You can't beat it. Remember, this doesn't have to be complicated, it just needs to be new. For example, if you normally grill your chicken, try roasting it, or frying it. If you normally have a baked potato, try a sweet potato. Remember, it is in having new experiences that we build confidence.

Are you still wondering how this builds confidence? Let's try a few experiences and see what clues you gain from this treasure hunt. Remember, log your experiences so you can remember what you learned.

Name of restaurant you went to: _____
Why did you choose this restaurant? _____
_____
List anyone who went with you: _____
How far was it from your house? _____
How did you get there? (drive, get a ride, bus, etc) _____
Was there a wait to eat when you arrived? _____
What type of seating did you have? _____
What was the weather like during this time? _____
_____

Was the temperature of the building comfortable? _____

What did you order? _____
_____

Did you enjoy the meal you ate? _____

What was one memorable moment? _____
_____
_____

Did anything happen that made you smile? _____
_____

Did anything happen that made you frown? _____
_____

One thing I want to remember during this experience: _____
_____
_____

Take a moment to think about this entire experience. While I hope this experience was positive, even if it was not fun, or the food was not good, my goal for you is that you learned something about yourself from going through this experience. And not only did you learn something, but you are willing to try again to see what happens the next time. Remember, confidence comes from practicing having experiences.

Write out your experience so you remember as you are trying other experiences:

_____
_____
_____
_____
_____
_____
_____
_____

Write down the next culinary experiences you want to have:

1. I will cook _____
2. I will cook _____
3. I will go to restaurant _____
4. I will go to restaurant _____

My attempt at a Spinach and Mushroom Omelet with bacon and strawberries
Jennifer Erickson

Write down what you learned from your second culinary experience. Include how this experience was different from your first experience. Additionally write down what you plan to do a little differently for your third experience, so that you learn something new.

Take a picture and paste it in here... or draw your own.

Five

Clue two – Get wild

With your first self-confidence clue you just completed, you were focused on food. Now, it's time to get wild. Does your city have a zoo, an aquarium, or an animal sanctuary of some type? From my research most cities do have some place like the ideas I listed if they are at least medium in size. A smaller city may not, in that case, you may need to go to the city next door. In Richmond, Virginia, we have the Richmond Metro Zoo in Chesterfield Virginia. This zoo is quite enjoyable, with different activities to do while walking around and seeing the animals.

Why do I want you to go to a zoo or aquarium? Because they are just a lot of fun. It can be so nice to be outside, breathing in the fresh air, and getting some gentle physical activity while walking. Stopping to watch the animals enjoying life instinctually can be very relaxing. You can relax, enjoy the outdoors at a zoo or a calming environment if you are at an aquarium. And it is so much easier to be confident if we are calm.

The secondary gain out of this clue is that you are most likely around people. You don't have to talk to anyone, but it is good to get used to being in public areas, ensuring you are comfortable navigating random areas with other people. If we don't get used to navigation with other random people, it can prevent us from going to concerts, festivals, or other community events.

Having a new experience, even at a zoo or aquarium, teaches us something about our self and that is what this treasure hunt is about. Make sure you pay attention to what you are thinking and how you are feeling as you go through your experience.

Zebra taking a stroll at the Richmond Metro Zoo, Chesterfield, VA
Photography by Jennifer Erickson

Name of the zoo or aquarium you went to: _____
_____
Why did you choose this location? _____
_____
_____
List anyone who went with you: _____
_____

How far was it from your house? _____
How did you get there? (drive, get a ride, bus, etc) _____
Was it worth the traveling to go to this location? _____
_____

Was there a wait to get in? _____
What was the weather like during this trip? _____
_____

What animal did you see first? _____
What animal was the most surprising (in any way)? _____
_____

Which was the stinkiest animal? _____
Which animal was the prettiest? _____
Was there anything else to do at this location (zipline, tram, etc)?
If yes, did you "do" the extra? _____
_____

Did you buy a souvenir? If yes, what? _____
What was one memorable moment? _____
_____

Did anything happen that made you smile? _____
_____

Did anything happen that made you frown? _____
_____

One thing I want to remember during this experience: _____
_____
_____

Take a moment to reflect about this entire experience. How was it? Did you get into it? Was there a time you were nervous? Was this easy? How was it being around other people you don't know. My goal for you is that you learned something about yourself from going through this experience. And not only did you learn something, but you are willing to try again to see what happens the next time. Remember, confidence comes from practicing engaging in experiences.

Write out your experience so you remember as you are trying other experiences:

_____
_____
_____
_____
_____
_____
_____
_____
_____
_____
_____
_____

Write down the next experience you will have so you can get wild:

1. I will go to _____
2. I will go to _____
3. I will go to _____

Write down what you want to learn about yourself during your next wild experience:

_____
_____
_____
_____
_____
_____
_____
_____

Take a picture and paste it in here... or draw your own.

Six

clue Three – smell the Flowers

Are you ready for your next adventure? This time we are going to stop and smell the flowers. No, not just anywhere. I want you to find a botanical garden, a community garden, or another place that has a large area of flowers. In Richmond, Virginia we have Lewis Ginter Botanical Garden, the gardens at Maymont, the E. Claiborne and Lora Robins Sculpture Garden at VMFA, the Agecroft Hall and Gardens, and The Enchanted Garden at the Poe Museum.

In each of these areas you have a chance to explore in a way that you haven't before. Our first experience was focused on food, a necessity of life. Our second experience was focused on observing animals in their natural setting. That experience also gave us a way to relax, being in the moment and not focus on everything else in our life. This experience will add to the first two.

Taking time to smell the flowers is important. It really isn't just about smelling them, but being out in nature, seeing the natural world, not just man-made things. You get to see how the flowers grow, which ones grow in which season, which ones grow tall and which ones stay small. You get to see the beauty in their dying or turning brown. I hope you enjoy this experience and the interactions you have with others who are also out enjoying the space as well.

Lewis Ginter Botanical Garden, Henrico, VA
Photography by Jennifer Erickson

Name of the place you went to: _____
_____
Why did you choose this location? _____
_____
List anyone who went with you: _____
How far was it from your house? _____
How did you get there? (drive, get a ride, bus, etc) _____
Was there a wait to get in? _____
What was the weather like during this trip? _____
If the weather was rainy or really warm, did it diminish the trip?
_____

Which flower did you see first? _____

Did you see a new flower that you had never seen before? If yes, which one? _____

Which flower was the prettiest to you, and why? _____
_____

Which flower was the ugliest to you, and why? _____
_____

Which flower smelled the best to you? _____

Did you see a lot of bumble bees? _____

Did you see many butterflies? _____

Was there anything extra at the location, such as lights, sculptures, or other displays to enhance the experience? If yes, what were they?
_____

What was one memorable moment? _____
_____

Did anything happen that made you smile? _____
_____

Did anything happen that made you frown? _____
_____

One thing I want to remember during this experience: _____
_____
_____
_____

Take a moment to reflect about this entire experience. How was it? Did it connect with you more than "it was just a place I went to see? Was there a time you were nervous? Was this easy? My goal for you is that you learned something about yourself from going through this experience. And not only did you learn something, but you found you gained something and are willing to try again to see what happens the next time. Remember, confidence comes from practicing new experiences.

Write out your experience so you remember as you are trying other experiences:

_____
_____
_____
_____
_____
_____
_____
_____
_____
_____
_____

Write down the next experience you will have so you can continue to smell the flowers:

1. I will go to _____
2. I will go to _____

Write down what you want to learn about yourself during your second flower experience:

_____
_____
_____
_____
_____
_____

TREASURE HUNT YOUR CITY | 27

Take a picture and paste it in here... or draw your own.

Seven

clue four – Step away from the Asphalt

Yep, its time to get off the asphalt. Now what I mean by stepping away from the asphalt is that we need to get away from the "roads" we drive every day. Depending on where you live, this might mean you head to the beach and walk in the sand. Or you might find a dirt trail and take a long walk. You might even find a combination.

We get so caught up either driving or getting driven from place to place. We go from home to work, and back home again. We stop at the grocery store, a department store, or a convenience store. We take care of our children, our fur babies, or maybe other family members.

Day in and day out we go go go. This fast paced life style is the quickest way to lose yourself and even your self-confidence because you don't have time to take in an experience, to reflect on it, to learn from it, and to think about what it means for you.

Virginia is known for its many outdoor options. Mountains in the west, beaches to the east, with dozens of state parks and trails in between. In Richmond, Virginia you might try going to Brown's Island or nearby Belle Isle. There is the Buttermilk Trail, Pony Pasture Rapids Trail, North Bank Trail, Forest Hill Park Trail, Rockwood Park Trails, James River Canal Walk, Byrd Park Trails, and many more. Many of the trails in Richmond are along or in view of water, so a great combination of different scenery.

First Landing State Park, Virginia Beach, VA
Photography by Jennifer Erickson

Name of the location you chose: _____

_____

Why did you choose this location? _____

_____
_____

List anyone who went with you: _____
How far was it from your house? _____
How did you get there? (drive, get a ride, bus, etc) _____
What was the weather like during this trip? _____

How long was this trip (in time or length)? _____

Have you even been to this trail/location before? _____

Would you go to this location again? And why or why not? _____
_____
_____

At this location, did you walk, sit, or do something else? _____
_____

Why did you select the activity above? _____
_____

What was one memorable moment? _____
_____

Did anything happen that made you smile? _____
_____

Did anything happen that made you frown? _____
_____

One thing I want to remember during this experience: _____
_____
_____

For your next trip, what would you do differently? _____
_____
_____

Does the season or weather impact what you might do next? _____
_____
_____

Take a moment to reflect about this entire experience. How was it? Did it connect with you more than "it was just a place I went to see? Was there a time you were nervous? Was this easy? My goal for you is that you learned something about yourself from going through this experience. And not only do I want you to learn something, but I'm hoping you are willing to try again to see what happens the next time. Remember, confidence comes from practicing new experiences.

Write out your experience so you remember as you are trying other experiences:

_____
_____
_____
_____
_____
_____
_____
_____
_____
_____
_____
_____

Write down the next experience you will have in this category so you can continue to step away from the asphalt:

1. I will go to _____
2. I will go to _____
3. I will go to _____

Write down what you want to learn about yourself during your second experience:

_____
_____
_____
_____
_____
_____
_____
_____
_____

Take a picture and paste it in here... or draw your own.

Eight

clue Five – Walk in History

Why walk in history, simple, it helps us take a look at our present. Taking a moment to pause and reflect on how life used to be is important. Reflecting on history not only teaches us about today, it teaches us about cultural changes, it helps us understand other people or groups, and it helps us make better decisions as citizens. No matter which state you live in, there are probably more museums than you realize.

In Richmond Virginia there are many museums. We have the Virginia Museum of Fine Arts, Children's Museum of Richmond, Virginia Museum of History and Culture, American Civil War Museum, Virginia Holocaust Museum, The Poe Museum, Maggie L. Walker National Historic Site, The Richmond Railroad Museum, and so many more.

When going to a museum I try to image what it was like for the painter, sculptor, the citizens living in that time period, and what the world was like at that time. After a bit, I will think about how much has changed, not just with art, culture, or events, but also as people in society. How have I changed because of these events or the people who have lived through these events.

Taking a walk in history is a chance to understand your own perceptions and misunderstandings. If I really invest my time in a museum or historical experience, I can never walk away feeling the same. I hope you have a similar experience. I hope that you embrace your experience and discover who you are, because of your/our collective past.

National D-Day Memorial, Bedford, VA
Photography by Jennifer Erickson

Name of the historical location you chose to go: _____
_____
Why did you choose this location? _____
_____
List anyone who went with you: _____
How far was it from your house? _____
How did you get there? (drive, get a ride, bus, etc) _____
What this an indoor or outdoor historical location? _____

If outdoor, what was the weather like during this trip? _____
_____

How much time did you spend at the location? _____
Had you even been to this location before? _____
_____

If you have been to this location before, did you have a deeper appreciation after the second time? _____
_____

Would you go to this location again? Why or why not? _____
_____

What was one memorable moment? _____
_____

Did anything happen that made you smile? _____
_____

Did anything happen that made you frown? _____
_____

One thing I want to remember during this experience: _____
_____
_____

For your next trip, what would you do differently as you prepare to go? _____
_____
_____

Take a moment to reflect about this historical experience. How was it? Did it connect with you more than "it was just a place I went to see? Was there a time you were nervous? Was this easy?

My goal for you is that you learned something about yourself from going through this experience. And not only do I want you to learn something, but I'm hoping you are willing to try again to see what happens the next time you step back in history. Remember, confidence comes from practicing new experiences.

Write out your experience so you remember as you are trying other experiences:

_____
_____
_____
_____
_____
_____
_____
_____
_____
_____

Write down the next experience you will have in this category so you can continue to walk in history:

1. I will go to _____
2. I will go to _____
3. I will go to _____

Write down what you want to learn about yourself during your second experience:

_____
_____
_____
_____
_____
_____
_____
_____
_____
_____

TREASURE HUNT YOUR CITY | 37

Take a picture and paste it in here... or draw your own.

Nine

Clue Six – wait for sunset

When is the last time you sat and watched the sun set? Heck, I'd take a sun rise for this clue. There is something very calming about sitting and genuinely observing the clouds go by. Then you wait patiently for that moment when you see the sun the colors in the sky start to change. A golden yellow and orange color against a blue sky. Then finally the sun drops below the horizon.

Or for you morning people; waking up and hearing the silence, sneaking outside so that you don't disturb anyone or the soft sounds of morning. Then you wait patiently to see the dawn of a new day. You sit still, watching patiently as the colors change while the sun slowly comes up over the horizon. The sky goes from dark to a soft light, then to an explosion of reds and oranges streaking across the sky.

Taking the time to watch the magic of the world move can remind you that the world does keep moving on. Whether you are having a nice or challenging week, the earth will keep turning, each day will keep passing. Taking this time can also remind you of the power and strength of the world. The thoughts and feelings you experience will be unique to you alone.

Sunset at the Roanoke Star, Roanoke, VA
Photography by Jennifer Erickson

Sunrise at Virginia Beach, VA
Photography by Jennifer Erickson

While many people report enjoying watching a rising sun or a setting sun, you won't know what it is like for you until you try it. And honestly, I would recommend trying both. Yes, if you are not a morning person, catching a rising sun might be hard, but it will be worth doing it at least once. Again, this treasure hunt is about having experiences and reflecting on how they impact you.

Did you watch the sun rise or set? _____

Where were you when you watched the sun rise or set? _____

_____

What type of location is this (home, park, beach, mountains, etc)?

_____

Why did you choose this location? _____

_____

List anyone who sat with you: _____

_____

If this was away from home, how did you get there? (drive, get a ride, bus, etc) _____

What was the weather like during your observation? _____

_____

Why did you pick sunrise/sunset over the other? _____

_____

How much time did you spend at the location after the sun came up or went down? _____

Had you even been to this location before? _____

Would you go to this location again? Why or why not? _____

_____

What was one memorable moment? _____

_____

Did anything happen that made you smile? _____

_____

Did anything happen that made you frown? _____

_____

One thing I want to remember during this experience: _____

_____

What words would you use to describe the experience? _____

_____

Take a moment to reflect about this experience. How was it? Did it connect with you more than "it was just an experience to have? Was this easy or challenging? Take time and keep reflecting. My goal for you is that you learned something about yourself from going through this experience. And not only do I want you to learn something, but I'm hoping you are willing to try again. Remember, confidence comes from practicing new experiences.

Write out your experience so you remember as you are trying other experiences:

_____
_____
_____
_____
_____
_____
_____
_____
_____
_____
_____
_____
_____

Write down the next time you will try a sunset or sunrise.

1. I will go to _____
2. I will go to _____

Write down what you want to learn about yourself during your second experience:

_____
_____
_____
_____
_____
_____
_____
_____
_____
_____
_____

Take a picture and paste it in here... or draw your own.

Ten

Clue Seven – Test a Hobby

It is interesting how many people I talk to that don't have a hobby. Now, having a hobby doesn't automatically make you confident, however, having a hobby does allow you to explore something fun and/or interesting without judgement. It also lets you focus on something outside of your job/career, being a husband or wife, a father or mother, a sibling, or any other role that you have. A hobby allows you to solely focus on yourself.

Don't let the idea of focusing "on you" sway you from this experience. I hear all the time that focusing on oneself is selfish. I say, "focusing on yourself is self-care". Let me explain what I mean. If I see people and say, "hey, look what I get to do", that might be considered bragging. But me taking time to do something that makes me happy, that is just self-care.

I have included a different picture for each chapter. This picture is me to demonstrate me trying a new hobby, sort of. My hobby is photography, typically landscapes. I also like gentle hiking (have to be kind to my knees). I will find ways to combine walks/hiking with photography. In fact, I will even travel some place and only spend 30 minutes there, just to take pictures. Sometimes we have to be adaptable and figure out how to try something even with limitations.

In fact, I am writing this workbook during the time period that the corona virus is effecting the world and our everyday life. My options for traveling are cut way down. Rather than just wait, I decided to try something new. Portrait photography. Some might ask if that is really something new. The answer: Absolutely! It is very much a different art type. I really have come to respect portrait photography.

Let's talk about what the word hobby means. The basic definition of hobby is an activity done regularly in one's leisure time for pleasure. What the definition does not say is that it has to be measured, it has to be the same thing, it has to cost money, or it has to be done alone or with someone. A hobby is just an activity that one does for pleasure. Its not complicated.

The difficult part might be, if you aren't sure what you like to do for pleasure. That happens to a lot of people. What I suggest then is to try several hobbies. Use Groupon to find deals. Ask friends what they do and just give it a try. You aren't trying to pick one that lasts forever, you are trying to find one or a few things that you enjoy when not working. Besides photography and walking/hiking, I enjoy arts/crafts, woodworking, going to museums, and many more. While I have a couple core hobbies. I will do other things on rainy days, or wintery cold day. Yuck. I like to do some of my hobbies when I'm alone and when I'm with friends. I sometimes go places that cost money and sometimes I go places that are free. I recommend you try several things and see how you feel after each one. That will help you learn more about yourself, which is the goal.

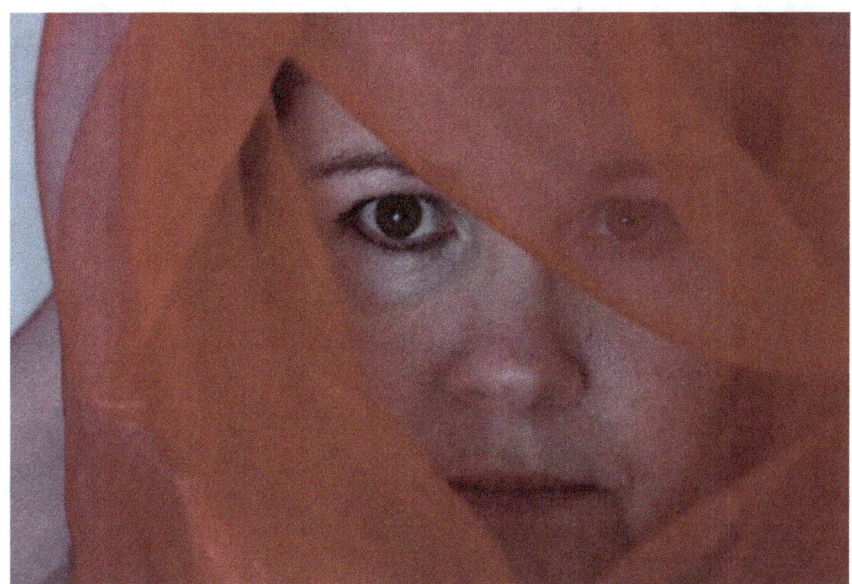

Portrait Practice - Self Picture
Photography by Jennifer Erickson

Name of the hobby you decided to try: _____
_____
Why did you choose this hobby? _____
_____
Is this a variation on something you already do? _____
_____
List anyone who helped you decide what to try: _____
Was it hard to decide what to try? _____
If yes, why? _____
_____
Did you have to leave your house to try the new hobby? _____
If yes, where did you go? _____
If you had to leave home, how did you get there? (drive, get a ride, bus, etc) _____
How much time did you spend on this hobby? _____
Is this a hobby where it will take days or weeks to work on? _____
_____

What was new about this experience for you? _____
_____
_____

Would you do this again? Why or why not? _____
_____

What was one memorable moment? _____
_____

Did anything happen that made you smile? _____
_____

Did anything happen that made you frown? _____
_____

One thing I want to remember during this experience: _____
_____
_____

For your next hobby, what would you do differently as you prepare?
_____
_____

Take a moment to reflect about this hobby experience. How was it? Did it connect with you more than "it was just a thing to try? Was there a time you were nervous? Was this easy? My goal for you is that you learned something about yourself from going through this experience. And not only do I want you to learn something, but I'm hoping you are willing to try again or motivated to try another hobby to see what happens the next time. Remember, confidence comes from practicing new experiences.

Write out your experience so you remember as you are trying other experiences:

_____
_____
_____
_____
_____

_____
_____
_____
_____
_____
_____
_____
_____
_____

Write down the next hobby you will test:

1. I will try: _____
2. I will try: _____
3. I will try: _____

Write down what you want to learn about yourself during your next experience:

_____
_____
_____
_____
_____
_____
_____
_____
_____
_____
_____

48 | JENNIFER ERICKSON, PH.D.

Take a picture and paste it in here... or draw your own.

Eleven

Clue Eight – find a quiet place

Are you wondering what I mean by a quiet place? I hope so because I want to talk about the idea of a quiet place. A quiet place is exactly what it sounds like and more. For the purposes of this treasure hunt you are trying to create a psychological atmosphere in the quiet space. What is a psychological atmosphere? It is defined as an individual's perception of their environment. For example, a psychological environment at work, where you feel emotionally bad, pressured, vulnerable, disrespected, etc can leave you feeling bad even when you leave the physical space of that job.

So this clue is more than just finding a quiet place, it is about finding a space (or creating one) that gives you an emotionally positive vibe. The picture here is at Lewis Ginter Botanical Garden. I enjoy going there to walk around by myself. I spend time looking at the flowers, the unique trees (like the one pictured), and I love breathing in the air there. I know cognitively or analytically that the air is no different than any other air. But for me, there is a psychological atmosphere where I can feel calm, at peace, quiet, and mindful.

Are you asking yourself, "if I already visited a quiet place like the sunset, or beach, or park, or another place as a clue, can I get a two-fer out of it"? The answer is no. Sorry, remember, part of your quest is having multiple experiences. So no two-fers. Besides, you might deprive yourself of a really great place if you don't try multiple areas.

I hope you are trying to come up with a list of places. A rule of thumb is, list two places that are free, two that cost money, two that would feel good doing alone, two that you can do with a friend, two places inside, and two places outside. This gives you several ideas and depending on the day you hunt for this clue, you don't have to do new research because of weather.

To get you started, some places in Richmond, Virginia might be the Virginia Fine Arts Museum (free, alone or with a friend, inside), canal walk near Brown's Island (free, alone or with a friend, outside), Pocahontas State Park (free, with a friend, outside), the Virginia Museum of History & Culture (fee, alone or with a friend, inside), a local park, your back yard, a walk in the rain (no lightning of course), or any place that makes you feel calm, relaxed, at peace, and able to smile. This is the perfect area to practice mindfulness as well.

Mindfulness is the practice of being present, in the moment, without personal judgement. Use a grounding technique to help you stay in the moment. Grounding is the process of linking yourself to the moment. Using your five sense is a good way to ground. Be aware of what you see, what you smell, what you hear, what you feel (physically), and if you have a food or drink, what you taste.

TREASURE HUNT YOUR CITY | 51

Lewis Ginter Botanical Garden, Henrico, VA
Photography by Jennifer Erickson

Name of the place you chose: _____
_____
Why did you choose this place? _____
_____
List anyone who went with you: _____
If you brought someone with you, were they able to appreciate the challenge in finding a quiet place? Or did they make it loud?
_____
_____

How far was it from your house? _____
How did you get there? (drive, get a ride, bus, etc) _____
Were you inside or out? _____
What was the weather at the place (if you were outside)? _____
_____

How much time did you spend at the place? _____
Had you even been to this place before? _____
Would you go to this place again? Why or why not? _____
_____

What was one memorable moment? _____

_____

What was it like to be in a quiet place? _____

_____

How long has it been since you were just quiet for a bit? _____

_____

Did anything happen that made you smile? _____

_____

Did anything happen that made you frown? _____

_____

What was the psychological atmosphere like at the place? _____

_____

_____

_____

_____

For your next trip, what would you do differently as you prepare to go?

_____

_____

_____

_____

_____

Take a moment to reflect about this quiet experience. How was it? Did it connect with you more than "it was just a thing to experience? Was there a time you were nervous? Was this easy? My goal for you is that you learned something about yourself from going through this experience. And not only do I want you to learn something, but I'm hoping you are willing to try again to see what happens the next time you find a quiet place. Remember, confidence comes from practicing new experiences.

Write out your experience so you remember as you are trying other experiences:

_____
_____
_____
_____
_____
_____
_____
_____
_____
_____
_____

Write down the next way you will find a quiet space so you can continue practicing creating a calming and peaceful psychological atmosphere:

1. I will go to _____
2. I will go to _____
3. I will go to _____

Write down what you want to learn about yourself during your second experience:

_____
_____
_____
_____
_____
_____
_____
_____

Take a picture and paste it in here... or draw your own.

Twelve

clue Nine – Go low Tech

With the increased use of technology in our daily lives, there is a need to go low tech from time to time. Now, don't worry, this is not an attempt to copy one of those meme's that ask, "could you live in a remote cabin for one month without any technology, if you knew you would get One Million Dollars". I think many people would struggle with that answer. From people who I have talked to, people would like to say yes, but know deep down it would be a struggle.

In our daily lives, we are high consumers of technology. It is in our homes, our cars, our jobs, and in many cases, in the way we relax. Now, don't get me wrong, I am not anti-technology. I love being high tech and all that the 21st Century has to offer with modern advancement. However, there is also a time to turn it off.

For this clue, there are many ways to engage in low tech. You can go camping for a weekend. In my picture, these are Yurts where I was camping. If you have never seen one, they are pretty neat. A yurt is a round tent. In Virginia there are a few state parks or vacation organizations that offer Yurts as an option different from your standard tent. Although a cabin or tent can be just as fun.

Yurt Camping in western Virginia
Photography by Jennifer Erickson

Additional low tech options without leaving home could be: board game night, interactive game night (charades), dice games (yahtzee), or card games (solitare, go fish, and more). There are many options for afternoon or evenings where we can let our phones, computers, and even televisions take a break.

Which low tech option did you go for? _____
Why did you choose this option? _____
_____
Is this an activity that you have done before? If yes, how recently?
_____
List anyone who participated with you: _____
Was it more fun doing this activity with a friend? _____
Why? _____
_____
Was this something you had to leave your house for? _____

If this was away from home, how did you get there? (drive, get a ride, bus, etc) _____

What was the weather like during your low-tech time? _____

_____

If the weather was bad, was it easier to go low tech? _____

_____

How much time did you spend doing this low-tech activity? _____

Could you have kept going or were you ready to stop? _____

_____

While you were away from technology (or had limited technology) did you miss it? _____

If you missed the technology, what do you think about that? _____

_____

What was one memorable moment? _____

_____

_____

Did anything happen that made you smile? _____

_____

Did anything happen that made you frown? _____

_____

One thing I want to remember during this experience: _____

_____

_____

What words would you use to describe the experience? _____

_____

Take a moment to reflect about this experience. How was it? Did it connect with you more than "it was just an experience to have? Was this easy or challenging? Take time and keep reflecting. My goal for you is that you learned something about yourself from going through this experience. And not only do I want you to learn something, but I'm hoping you are willing to try again. Remember, confidence comes from practicing new experiences.

Write out your experience so you remember as you are trying other experiences:

_____
_____
_____
_____
_____
_____
_____
_____
_____
_____
_____
_____
_____

Write down what low-tech activity you will try next time.

1. I will try _____
2. I will try _____

Write down what you want to learn about yourself during your second low-tech experience:

_____
_____
_____
_____
_____
_____
_____
_____
_____

Take a picture and paste it in here... or draw your own.

Thirteen

clue Ten – See the world Differently

When is the last time you stopped to see the world differently? Are you wondering what I mean by this? Let me explain. There are many times that we are so caught up in doing our "normal" daily thing, that we forget to step outside of that and try something completely different.

It's pretty normal, I was that way once in my life. I would get up, eat breakfast, get kids ready for school, get them to school, I'd go to work, work all day, come home, cook dinner for everyone, make sure kids did homework, have an hour to collect my thoughts (or clean up the kitchen, do laundry, etc). Then I'd started getting kids ready for bed, sometimes I'd even work from home because of the type of job I had. And then I'd finally go to bed. And repeat Monday through Friday. Weekends consisted of chores, kids' things, maybe sleeping in occasionally, and squeezing in my own fun. I can say I probably had a decade where the only time something was different was during my one-week vacation.

I could have set up my life a little different even with kids, but I didn't realize I could. I didn't realize that some weekends should be equally about me (or my husband) as it was the kids. But once I finally realized I could do things differently I started, which is why I now love helping people learn the same thing. So again, what does it mean to see the world differently.

Blue Ridge Mountains, Virginia
Photography by Jennifer Erickson

"A City Girl in the Mountains"

I mean doing things that you have never done that are very much out of your norm. Do you like listening to music, why not go take a Ballroom Dancing lesson. You don't have to become an expert but learn to experience music in a different way. If you love going to the beach, then go to the mountains (or a desert) and see the horizon a different way. Do you love the warmth of summer, then plan to do something in the cold of winter. Are you a social butterfly, then go do something alone. Do you live at sea level, then head to the mountains. Do you live in a city, then travel to a small town (or vice versa). Do you love art, then try something with technology. See the world in a very different way. One note: you could say that the experience of sunset and sunrise would fit into this category, but since there is no double dipping, you need to find something else.

Try anything that is very different from your normal routine. Try to image what it would be like to live in another way.

Name the location or thing you chose to try: _____
Why did you choose this thing? _____
_____
List anyone who went with you: _____
How far was it from your home? _____
How did you get there? (drive, get a ride, bus, etc) _____
What was the weather like during this experience? _____
How much time did you spend at the experience? _____
Had you even done something like this before? _____
Would you do this again? Why or why not? _____
_____
What was one memorable moment? _____
_____
Did anything happen that made you smile? _____
_____
Did anything happen that made you frown? _____
_____
One thing I want to remember during this experience: _____
_____
_____
For your next trip, what would you do differently as you prepare to go? _____
_____

Take a moment to reflect about this new experience. How was it? Did it connect with you more than "it was just a thing to do to complete the workbook? Was there a time you were nervous? Was this easy? My goal for you is that you learned something about yourself from going through this experience. And not only do I want you to learn something, but I'm hoping you are willing to try again to see what happens the next time you try to see the world differently. Remember, confidence comes from practicing new experiences.

Write out your experience so you remember as you are trying other experiences:

_____
_____
_____
_____
_____
_____
_____
_____
_____
_____
_____

Write down the next experience you will have so that you can see the world differently:

1. I will go to _____
2. I will go to _____
3. I will go to _____

Write down what you want to learn about yourself during your second experience:

_____
_____

_____
_____
_____
_____
_____
_____
_____
_____
_____
_____
_____
_____
_____

Take a picture and paste it in here... or draw your own.

Fourteen

clue ELEVEN – be fruity

I hope you like this next clue, its sweet (trying to be puny). The goal is to find some places in your city or in your state that you haven't been that involves food and adventure. The picture here is of a peach tree. I went to a Peach Orchard just outside of Charlottesville, Virginia where I was able to walk around and pick my own peaches. Later during the visit, I picked blueberries.

Are you asking yourself, "how will this create more self-confidence?" Well, again, it is the experience of going someplace new, doing something new, and reflecting on the experience. It is about having opinions, knowing what you like and what you're doing. Your self-awareness is growing with each experience.

Why fruit, because it also gives you something new to try when you get home. Have you ever made a peach pie, peach cobbler, or peach jam? Don't they all sound yummy. Don't limit yourself though to just fruit. Veggies can be a fun thing to go get as well. Have you been to a pumpkin patch to find your pumpkin rather than buying from a local grocery store? You can also support local farmers markets by purchasing fruits and veggies from them. This activity is a win win in many ways, which will hopefully make you smile.

Chiles Peach Orchard, Crozet, VA
Photography by Jennifer Erickson

When is the last time you roasted broccoli, or grilled asparagus, or even baked a squash? Veggies can be just as tasty and fun as fruits. Also, both fruits and veggies allow us to get to know food in many different natural forms and colors.

Do you find you only eat food one way? For example, mashed potatoes. When is the last time you baked them or fried them in slices? Do you always eat your carrots cooked, why not try them raw. What about snap peas. They are so tasty cold.

Take this opportunity to explore food, try it in different forms. Bake it, grill it, roast it and steam it. Try it hot, and then try it cold. What colors do you like looking at the most? Food is such an important aspect to our lives; it should be one that we are more invested in. We should enjoy food for its nutrition, but also for the enjoyment it brings from plate that has greens, reds, and oranges. I hope this chapter allows you to not only do something different but learn several new things about yourself.

Name of the fruit or veggie you went to pick/find: _____

Why did you choose this food? _____

List anyone who went with you: _____
How far was it from your house? _____
How did you get there? (drive, get a ride, bus, etc) _____
What was the weather like during this trip? _____
How much time did you spend at the location? _____
Had you even been to this location before? _____
Would you go to this location again? Why or why not? _____

What was one memorable moment? _____

Did anything happen that made you smile? _____

Did anything happen that made you frown? _____

What did you do with the food you went to go get? _____

One thing I want to remember during this experience: _____

For your next trip, what would you do differently as you prepare to go? _____

Take a moment to reflect about this food experience. How was it? Did it connect with you more than "it was just a thing I had to do? Was there a time you were nervous? Was this easy? My goal for you is that you learned something about yourself from going through this experience. And not only do I want you to learn something, but I'm hoping you are willing to try again to see what happens the next time you step back in history. Remember, confidence comes from practicing new experiences.

Write out your experience (both getting the food and what you did with it) so you remember as you are trying other foods:

_____
_____
_____
_____
_____
_____
_____
_____
_____
_____
_____
_____

Write down the next food you will go find and then eat:

1. Fruit: _____
2. Fruit: _____
3. Veggie: _____
4. Veggie: _____

Write down what you want to learn about yourself during your next experience:

_____
_____
_____
_____

TREASURE HUNT YOUR CITY | 69

_____
_____
_____
_____
_____
_____
_____
_____
_____
_____

Take a picture and paste it in here... or draw your own.

Fifteen

Clue twelve – find your Season

This was one of my favorite experiences I gave to myself. Yes, to completely do this one well, it actually takes an entire year. As I have mentioned in other chapters, we get so caught up in our daily lives, what we think we "should" be doing based on "societies" ideas, and what movies tell us we should do, that we sometimes don't take the time to really learn what we should be doing to actually be happy. So, for this hunt, we are going to take the time to discover which season we love the best.

For me personally, I am a three-season person. I really enjoy Spring, Summer, and Fall. I could give up Winter. I don't want to give up the winter holidays because they are social and focus on really good values, but snowy, wintery-mix, icy days. Yeah, I could leave those behind for the rest of my life. No judgement for people who love snow, I used to live in a northern state. I can appreciate the fun I used to have, but as we all do, I have changed.

So, the question is, what season are you? Have you really taken the time to pay attention? You might think to yourself, yeah, I do know my favorite season. I still think you should go through this exercise. Also, one thing to consider. Make sure when you do this exercise, you are doing it in the present and not the past. I've met people who will say "I love Winter because of Christmas, because my parents would decorate the house and sing songs when I was 10 years old".

My response is, that sounds like a wonderful experience as a child, but is that who you are now? Do you live that life now? Some times the reason why we loved (past tense) a season, is not necessarily the reason we love (present tense) it now. Make sure you are asking yourself, "how do I feel now about this season." Here we are going to play a game and then your treasure hunt will come from testing everything out.

Answer the following:
What is your favorite clothing and why? _____

What is your favorite "extra" (scarf, hat, gloves, warm socks) and why? _____
What is your perfect temperature (with clothing on) and why? ___
_____

What is your favorite style of concert (arena, small pub/bar, field/outdoor) and why? _____
_____

What is your favorite type of festival and why? _____
_____

What is your favorite outdoor activity and why? _____
_____

What is your favorite indoor activity and why? _____
_____

What is your favorite holiday and why? _____
_____

What is your favorite vacation spot and why? _____
_____
_____

Spring in the Japanese Gardens, Maymont - Richmond, VA
Photography by Jennifer Erickson

We went through several questions to help you discover many of your favorites. Did you see any patterns emerging? For example, favorite outdoor activity, festival, clothing, etc. Did you learn you like Fall festivals or Summer parties? What did you learn about yourself? It is now time to test a season, confirm if you are accurate in how you feel about your favorites.

What season are you in now? _____
What are some of the favorites you thought of that match the current season? _____
_____
_____

What activity are you doing to confirm you enjoy this season? _____

Why did you choose this activity? _____

List anyone who went with you: _____

How far was it from your house? _____
How did you get there? (drive, get a ride, bus, etc) _____

What was the weather like during this activity? _____

How much time did you spend at this activity? _____
How long has it been since you did this activity or was it brand new?
_____

Would you do this again? Why or why not? _____

What was one memorable moment? _____

Did anything happen that made you smile? _____

Did anything happen that made you frown? _____

Out of the four seasons, is this one favorite or least favorite or in the middle? _____

Did you learn anything new about yourself as it relates to the seasons: _____
_____
_____

Will you try something else this season to confirm your beliefs?
_____
_____

Write out your experience so you remember as you are trying other experiences:

_____
_____
_____
_____
_____

Write down the next experience you will plan for this season. Start thinking about the next season and repeat this exercise.

1. This season I will: _____
2. Next season I will: _____
3. Next season I will: _____

Write down what you want to learn about yourself during your next experience:

_____
_____
_____
_____
_____
_____
_____
_____
_____
_____
_____
_____
_____
_____
_____

Take a picture and paste it in here... or draw your own.

Sixteen

finding your TREASURE

Congratulations on getting to the end of the workbook. I hope you found your treasure chest. Remember the treasure inside will be a little different for each person. My wish for you is that through all of the different experiences, you learned some new and/or interesting things about yourself and more importantly, that you gained some self-confidence.

Always remember to try new things, whether the outcome is fun or boring, easy or difficult, you will learn something new about yourself just from going through it. And confidence grows from experience. I believe this is the best win win you will find.

While this is the last chapter, your treasure hunt does not have to stop. This workbook was designed to help you get started on your self-confidence journey, but you are encouraged to keep it going. It is through new experiences, self-discovery, and experiencing change that you will continue to grow self-confident. Self-discovery is something you should continue throughout your life. In fact, use annual celebrations like birthdays, New Year's, or anniversaries as reminders to ask yourself: "Have I done anything new lately"?

Before you start the next phase, take a moment to reflect on this entire Treasure Hunt:

How long did it take you to complete the workbook? _____
_____

Do you feel you pushed yourself too much, that you didn't push yourself enough, or were you pretty good about finding your middle ground? _____
_____

Which type of experience was most challenging for you? And Why?
_____
_____

Which type of experience do you think you learned the most from and why?
_____
_____

Did the experiences help you confirm your likes and dislikes, so that if in the future someone tries to tell you how you should think or feel, you can confidently advocate for what you know?
Explain: _____
_____
_____
_____

Did the experiences help you visualize who you want to be? Explain:

_____
_____
_____

If you were very nervous, anxious, or scared during any of the new experiences, and you were able to complete them; what did you learn from being scare and pushing on?

_____
_____
_____
_____
_____

If you were very nervous, anxious, or scared during any of the new experiences, and you were not able to complete them, do you feel like you might be able to try again?

_____
_____
_____
_____

Did you find that going through these different experiences allowed you to personally grow?

If yes, in what way _____
_____
_____
_____

If no, did this spark any new ideas that might help you grow personally? How:

_____
_____

_____
_____
_____

Would you recommend to any friends, going through something like this? Why?

_____
_____
_____
_____
_____
_____
_____
_____

I want to take this final paragraph and say Congratulations. Whether you enjoyed the new experiences or not, the fact is you stuck with the process and completed the workbook. You should be proud of yourself. If you found that during the new experiences you were highly agitated or stressed, please consider talking to a counselor or therapist to help give you support as you continue your journey. It may just mean that you need a little more one on one help.

If you completed this workbook and found it helpful, then share the concept with a friend who is struggling with self-confidence. I'm really very excited about helping others and I hope you feel the same way. Struggling with self-confidence is what keeps us stuck and can hold us back. Now remember, if you pass on this suggestion, you don't want to help more than that. Like yourself, they have to go on their own journey of discovery. They may invite you to go with, but they need to be in charge.

I wish you all the best.

Jennifer Erickson is a Health Psychologist. She received her doctorate from Walden University, which is where she also received her master's in Mental Health Counseling. Jennifer used her passion for personal wellness in her dissertation which focused on using video public service announcements to motivate people to engage in physical activity. Jennifer has always been interested in motivation to create personal change.

Jennifer Erickson, Ph.D.

Jennifer changed career mid-life so that she could focus more on coaching, mentoring, and helping. She often shares this to promote the idea that we are never stuck in one place and never too old to make changes in our life. Prior to changing careers, Jennifer worked for 20 plus years in Healthcare Administration, 17 of which were in management or supervisory positions.

While Jennifer has worked with many clients in different settings and with different concerns, she has always focused on anxiety and personal wellness. The passion for helping people with anxiety has come from knowing many people who struggle with anxiety and fears in both personal and professional settings. Additionally knowing so many people in personal and professional settings where stress is so high that it significantly affects their lives and health.

When Jennifer is not coaching or mentoring, she can be found engaging in her favorite self-care activities; writing, hiking, traveling, and taking pictures. In fact, all the pictures provided in this workbook were taken by Jennifer. She encourages everyone to take the time to explore and find their treasure that comes from living a more self-confident and authentic life. Never be afraid to set boundaries, know your values, and be as authentic as possible.

www.ingramcontent.com/pod-product-compliance
Lightning Source LLC
Chambersburg PA
CBHW051409290426
44108CB00015B/2215